Biblical Forgiveness

Are There Two Types?

Ray Foucher

TEACH Services, Inc.
PUBLISHING
www.TEACHServices.com

World rights reserved. This book or any portion thereof may not be copied or reproduced in any form or manner whatever, except as provided by law, without the written permission of the publisher, except by a reviewer who may quote brief passages in a review.

This book was written to provide truthful information in regard to the subject matter covered. The author assumes full responsibility for the accuracy of all facts and quotations as cited in this book. The opinions expressed in this book are the author's personal views and interpretation of the Bible, and/or contemporary authors and do not necessarily reflect those of TEACH Services, Inc.

This book is sold with the understanding that the publisher is not engaged in giving spiritual, legal, medical, or other professional advice. If authoritative advice is needed, the reader should seek the counsel of a competent professional.

To view the author's Web site, visit http://www.tsibooks.com/foucher.

Copyright © 2013 TEACH Services, Inc.
ISBN-13: 978-1-57258-946-9 (Paperback)
ISBN-13: 978-1-57258-947-6 (ePub)
ISBN-13: 978-1-57258-948-3 (Kindle/Mobi)

All scripture quotations, unless otherwise indicated, are taken from the King James Version Bible.

Scripture quotations marked "NKJV™" are taken from the New King James Version®. Copyright © 1982 by Thomas Nelson, Inc. Used by permission. All rights reserved.

Scripture quotations marked NASB are taken from the New American Standard Bible®, Copyright © 1960, 1962, 1968, 1971, 1972, 1973, 1975, 1977, 1995 by The Lockman Foundation. Used by permission.

Scripture quotations marked BBE are taken from the Bible in Basic English, printed in 1965 by Cambridge Press in England. Public Domain.

Published by
TEACH Services, Inc.
P U B L I S H I N G
www.TEACHServices.com

Part 1: Introduction

Are you seeking forgiveness? Have you ever struggled with knowing whether or not God has forgiven you? In your relationship with God, do you feel forgiven? Or do you feel guilty? Do you know what the effects of guilty feelings are on emotional health? They are not good. Health and forgiveness are definitely related. Guilt produces emotional pain and can even result in physical disease. If you are struggling to know how to overcome guilt, then forgiveness is something you need to understand and seek after. But do we really understand what forgiveness is and how to get it?

How do you think God regards you when you sin? Is He upset? Does He have to be appeased or reconciled to you? Do you beg God to forgive you? Do you ever wonder if He does forgive you? In the world, and to a degree, even in Christianity, there is confusion over this topic.

If you do feel guilty and are carrying a load of guilt, a burden you would dearly like to be rid of, this study of forgiveness will provide you with the answer. Biblical forgiveness is the real solution to guilt, and understanding how forgiveness works, especially from God's perspective, can be a great help.

Let's start by examining what guilt is. A dictionary definition of guilt might be something like: "the fact or state of having done wrong." However, guilt is much more than a fact or state of being. Feelings are very much involved. Usually there is a feeling of estrangement or separation from the person we have wronged. We feel as though we are out of favor with them, and we suppose that they must feel anger toward us. There are often feelings of shame as well. Shame, while different from guilt, is often closely related.

Think about your own experiences with guilt and forgiveness and you will realize that forgiveness is indeed a two-party transaction. There are always at least two individuals involved. With God, we tend to think that we ask for forgiveness and if God feels like it He forgives us, and only then has forgiveness happened. The process is a little more involved than that, and this beautiful truth will give you a much better understanding of guilt, will make you feel a lot better about the process, and will help you considerably in dealing with your feelings of guilt.

Our translations of words from original languages sometimes do not retain all of the original meaning. This has happened here. There is a Greek word, *charizomai*, that refers to forgiveness as felt by the forgiver, the one doing the forgiving. On the other side of the two-party transaction, there are two Greek words, *apheimi* and *apoluo*, that describe what is happening within the person being forgiven. This study examines the meanings and uses of these words and will give you a much better understanding of how forgiveness works. You will understand the deficiency of the standard definition of guilt and see how freely forgiveness is offered to you.

God loves everyone far more than we can imagine. He always forgives every sin in the sense that He does not hold our sins against us. He is not angry with us. He does not love or care for us any less. *Charizomai* (often translated forgiveness) is the Greek word that describes His feelings of forgiveness toward us.

Whether you feel it or not, whether you even know it or not, God forgives you. You don't have to earn forgiveness from God, just accept it. When you realize His love and acceptance, then you will feel forgiven in your heart. What happens on your side of the forgiveness process—in your heart—is described by the words *apheimi* and *apoluo*. Remember, a child does not have to earn the love of his parents; it is freely given.

Jesus, who always said and did what was consistent with His Father's character, said as He was being crucified, "Father, forgive (*apheimi*) them." He wasn't asking His Father to feel like forgiving them (*charizomai*). Rather, He was asking that the soldiers mistreating Him could be lead to feel forgiven.

Of course, there is another aspect to forgiveness—the legal one—that involves our acceptance of the payment for the penalty of our sins. This is often described in terms such as the "blotting out" of sins. When we have a better understanding of God's love and His accepting attitude toward us, it makes it easy also to accept Jesus' sacrifice on our behalf so that our sins are covered in the legal sense. We then have the free gift of salvation and a title to heaven as well as a clear conscience and freedom from guilt. What a burden is lifted from our minds!

Part 1: Introduction

It Takes Two for Forgiveness to Happen

We need to understand that forgiveness is a transaction between two parties. In forgiveness, there is the **forgiver**, the one who offers and gives the pardon, and there is the **forgivee**, the one who accepts and receives the pardon. Forgiveness isn't just God forgiving us, but a process by which He forgives us, we receive and accept that forgiveness, and as a result, we feel forgiven. Let's try to understand forgiveness by looking at various scriptures that describe forgiveness from the perspective of both the forgiver and the forgivee. What does the Bible say about it?

Following is a step-by-step examination of what the Bible says about the topic and the process of forgiveness. We will look at the words in the original languages that are translated as "forgiveness" and related terms and see how the Bible itself uses the words in context. By allowing the Bible to define its own terms, we can come closer to understanding the original intent of the biblical teaching on this important topic. This study will help you understand the process of forgiveness and give you an appreciation for the Bible's ability to explain itself.

Part 2: The Definition of Forgiveness

To better understand the definition of forgiveness, let's examine what is happening on the side of each party involved in the forgiveness transaction. We will also look at what the Bible says about it and how the words translated as "forgiveness" are involved. I'll share a few quotes about forgiveness to illustrate the confusion and then we will do a word study. I hope you will be better able to understand the biblical definition for forgiveness, especially if you are dealing with guilt.

First, consider these verses: "But they and our fathers dealt proudly, and hardened their necks, and hearkened not to thy commandments, And refused to obey ... but thou art a God ready to pardon ..." (Neh. 9:16, 17).

In this passage has God's forgiveness already been given to them? No, He is "ready to pardon," as though He is about to do so. That means, at the point of writing, He hadn't done it yet. Perhaps He was waiting for them to do something.

What is commonly understood to happen before God administers forgiveness? Repentance and confession. Then God's forgiveness will be granted; He will pardon and bless.

Maybe this doesn't match your definition of the forgiveness process, or maybe it does. Yet what is the common understanding of God's attitude toward us before we repent and confess, and before He has forgiven us? Perhaps that He is angry or upset with us. And what is the attitude of God toward us (as commonly understood) after we repent? Probably that He is happy with us, favorable toward us, and ready to bless us. Basically, He is ready to pardon, we repent and "'fess up," and then He is ready to bless us. Is this really how it is? Does this correspond to your understanding of and definition for forgiveness? Consider the second verse: "Or despisest thou the riches of his goodness and forbearance and longsuffering; not knowing that the goodness of God leadeth thee to repentance?" (Rom. 2:4).

Which comes first according to this verse, the goodness of God or something on our part? The goodness of God. If the goodness of God leads us to repentance, then His goodness must come first. Confession and repentance follow His goodness.

Part 2: The Definition of Forgiveness

Now look at the third verse: "If we confess our sins, he is faithful and just to forgive us our sins, and to cleanse us from all unrighteousness" (1 John 1:9).

Which comes first according to this verse: our confession or His forgiveness? Our confession. This verse seems to require a clear precondition for forgiveness. When we have confessed our sins, then and only then do we receive forgiveness. It seems that God is holding something back from us until we meet a condition. Confession comes first, then forgiveness.

Couldn't this be confusing? In the first text, it sounds like God is ready to forgive once we repent and confess. In the second text, the goodness of God first leads us to confess and repent. According to the third text, if we confess, then He will forgive. "If" sounds like a precondition to me. Then we have a couple of verses that go back the other way: "For God so loved the world, that he gave his only begotten Son, that whosoever believeth in him should not perish, but have everlasting life" (John 3:16).

Indeed, He gave His Son before I came along and needed forgiveness.

"But God commendeth his love toward us, in that, while we were yet sinners, Christ died for us" (Rom. 5:8).

These verses suggest that God loved the world before He gave His Son to die for it, which suggests no precondition.

So which is it? Does He love us but not forgive us? Does He forgive us only as we meet conditions? And if He has not forgiven us, what is His attitude toward us? Does God's attitude toward us change when we sin? Do we need to pray earnestly so that God will change His attitude toward us, so that He will no longer ignore, reject, or punish us, and so that He will forgive us?

In looking at just a few scriptures to come up with a definition for forgiveness, we have seen seemingly contradictory statements that could be used in a definition of forgiveness. These verses have caused debate and misunderstanding. We know that the Word of God does not really contradict itself, so let's take a look at some of these apparent contradictions, explore the meaning of forgiveness, and see if we can better understand this topic. The benefits may not only be a better understanding of the subject but also a clearer conscience and a better appreciation of the plan of God and of His great love for us.

The Bible actually talks about two related but different events or processes when using the word "forgiveness." This word in the Bible is actually translated from several different Hebrew and Greek words with different meanings. We become confused because we have only one English word, which does not cover the shades of meaning in the original languages. As we study forgiveness further, we find that there is good news. A complete understanding of the definition of forgiveness is a great help in dealing with guilt, and it is very good news indeed.

Part 3: How is Forgiveness Normally Understood?

Carefully examining Bible verses on forgiveness can help us understand the meanings of the different words translated as "forgiveness" in both the Old Testament and the New Testament. We will look at several Bible verses on forgiveness and at some examples of how they are used. Because forgiveness is a two-party transaction, as I have already mentioned, we will look at forgiveness one side at a time.

First we will consider forgiveness as it applies to the forgivee, the one who is forgiven. The first word we want to look at is the Hebrew word *nasa* (Strong's H5375).[1] *Nasa* is used in the sense of bearing a load, lifting up, or taking away. Below are the uses and shades of meaning as given by the Online Bible.[2]

Uses: bear up, lift up, etc. 219; bear 115; take 58; bare 34; carry 30; take away, carry away 22; borne 22; armourbearer 18; forgive 16; accept 12; exalt 8; regard 5; obtained 4; respect 3; misc 74. Total: 654.

Meanings:
- to lift, bear up, carry, take
- to lift, lift up
- to bear, carry, support, sustain, endure
- to take, take away, carry off, forgive
- to cause one to bear (iniquity)
- to cause to bring, have brought

Let's look at some examples of the use of the word *nasa*.

"Thou hast forgiven the iniquity of thy people, thou hast covered all their sin" (Ps. 85:2).

This seems to carry the meaning we normally associate with Bible verses on forgiveness. God has taken away the sins of the people so they don't have to bear them.

"And if a soul sin, and commit any of these things which are forbidden

---

1 Strong's Concordance is a resource that numbers and defines each word in the Bible as an aid in understanding word meanings. The "H" or "G" preceding a number indicates the language: Hebrew or Greek.
2 All Hebrew and Greek word definitions in this study are from the Online Bible version 4.24, www.onlinebible.net. The number of occurrences for each word is for the Authorized KJV.

to be done by the commandments of the LORD; though he wist it not, yet is he guilty, and shall bear his iniquity" (Lev. 5:17).

Here *nasa* is translated "bear" as in carrying a load or bearing a burden. What the sinner is really bearing is the result of his iniquity, which could include the guilt, shame, and natural consequences of the sin. This is a burden that can largely be lifted by forgiveness.

"Look upon mine affliction and my pain; and forgive all my sins" (Ps. 25:18).

In this verse the removal of affliction and pain is associated with the forgiveness of sins. What sort of affliction and pain is this verse talking about? I think it would mainly be a hurting conscience; although if we could really know how it works, I believe we would find that there is a considerable connection between sin and a guilty conscience and physical disease.

"Blessed is he whose transgression is forgiven, whose sin is covered" (Ps. 32:1).

The result of *nasa* forgiveness is that the one forgiven is blessed or happy. There is a good result for the forgivee. These uses include the concept of taking something away from the forgivee.

The next Hebrew word we will look at is *calach* (Strong's H5545).

Uses: forgive 19; forgiven 13; pardon 13; spare 1. Total: 46.

Meanings:
- to forgive, pardon
- to be forgiven

Let's see how *calach* is used in Bible verses on forgiveness.

"Who forgiveth all thine iniquities; who healeth all thy diseases" (Ps. 103:3).

From this verse all we learn is that it is God who does the forgiving. He is the forgiver. Interestingly, in this verse there is a connection between being forgiven and healing.

"Let the wicked forsake his way, and the unrighteous man his thoughts: and let him return unto the Lord, and he will have mercy upon him; and to our God, for he will abundantly pardon" (Isa. 55:7).

This verse is similar to one of the Bible verses on forgiveness that we looked at earlier. It is saying that man first forsakes his own sinful way and returns to God, then God will pardon or forgive.

"It may be that the house of Judah will hear all the evil which I purpose to do unto them; that they may return every man from his evil way; that I may forgive their iniquity and their sin" (Jer. 36:3).

Again, people return from their evil way and as a result they are forgiven. (This sounds like something out of the book of Jonah, in which this happened to the whole city of Ninevah.)

"We have transgressed and have rebelled: thou hast not pardoned" (Lam. 3:42).

In this case, since they have transgressed or sinned and have rebelled rather than repented, God has not pardoned. Both of these two words, *nasa* and *calach*, include the meaning of taking something away. When you receive forgiveness, what is taken away from you? Guilt, shame, and debt. Can you see that these words are describing what is happening on the side of the forgivee?

Then we also have two similar New Testament words that are used in Bible verses on forgiveness. The first is *aphiemi* (Strong's G863).

Uses: leave 52; forgive 47; suffer 14; let 8; forsake 6; let alone 6; misc 13. Total: 146.

Meanings:
- to send away [the guilt]
- to permit, allow, not to hinder, to give up a thing to a person
- to leave, go way from one

Here is an example of the use of the word *aphiemi*: "And, behold, they brought to him a man sick of the palsy, lying on a bed: and Jesus seeing their faith said unto the sick of the palsy; Son, be of good cheer; thy sins be forgiven thee" (Matt. 9:2).

According to this verse, in whom who is the change taking place? Is it a change in God or in the sick man? What would be taken away from this man? Remember, the word *aphiemi* is used here, meaning shame, guilt, and so on.

The second Greek word, *apoluo* (Strong's G630) means much the same, as it is along the lines of "to set free," "to release."

"And they held their peace. And he took him, and healed him, and let him go" (Luke 14:4).

These Hebrew and Greek words refer to the work God accomplishes in the heart or mind of the believer through the merits of the death of Jesus. This forgiveness deals with the "canceling out" of sin's consequences. The Bible verses on forgiveness we have looked at in this part have described forgiveness from the viewpoint of the forgivee, the one who is forgiven. In the next part, we will examine additional Bible verses on forgiveness in which we will consider the viewpoint of the forgiver.

Part 4: Forgiveness in the Bible

What we have considered so far is forgiveness as it applies to the forgivee, the one who is forgiven. Now let's look at the other half of this two-party transaction and observe what is happening on the part of the forgiver. Remember, we are the forgivees, God is the forgiver. Let's examine what takes place in God's heart—on the level of His emotions—and at how God feels toward us as sinners.

Consider again John 3:16: "For God so loved the world, that he gave his only begotten Son, that whosoever believeth in him should not perish, but have everlasting life."

We see that the gift of God's Son to die for us was preceded by a love that already existed in God's heart toward sinners. This forgiveness did not originate at the cross; it was already there before Jesus' sacrifice. Had it not been for God's preexisting love for us, the events of the cross would never have taken place. It was because of God's love for the world that He gave us His only Son. This is a vital point because many believe that God would have continually retained malice toward man in His heart if it had not been for the cross. Many teach that it was through the cross that God was appeased of His enmity or hard feelings toward man. However, the cross did not bring about a change in God's emotional response toward us; rather, it displayed God's heartfelt sentiments for man, which He had held long before the events of the cross took place. Notice another passage that speaks of God's intrinsic forgiveness: "In whatever our heart condemns us; ... God is greater than our heart, and knows all things" (1 John 3:20, NASB).

We have all experienced that nagging feeling deep inside after we've done something we know to be wrong, have we not? The apostle John reminds us that when we are conscience stricken and wrestling under a weight of guilt, we are not to think the condemnation comes from God. God is greater than the heart. Although our hearts, our consciences, do condemn us, His spirit of forgiveness and love is already working to win us back from sin's consequences. The *Seventh-day Adventist Bible Commentary*, volume 7, paraphrases 1 John 3:19, 20 as follows:

"By genuinely loving our brother we may know that we are children of the truth, or of God. This knowledge will enable us to stand confidently in the presence of God, for even though our heart condemns us, since we are still sinners, we know that God is greater than our heart, His knowledge and understanding far surpass our own, and He is able to perceive our sincerity and to allow for the mistakes into which we fall."

He allows for our mistakes in that He has made provision for it. Long ago, I learned a little trick that has helped me through life. Maybe you've learned this as well. The trick is to not beat yourself up emotionally when you do something wrong, make a bad decision, or really mess up big time. We are human; we will make mistakes. You may have to suffer some consequences because of mistakes, but admit that you are not perfect, make it right in whatever way is needed, and get on with your life. I believe God wants us to do that; He doesn't want us carrying burdens around. He has forgiven us, and He wants us to forgive ourselves.

Let's look at the story in John chapter 8 of the woman taken in adultery. Jesus, after saying to her accusers, "He that is without sin among you, let him first cast a stone at her," wrote with His finger on the ground. It is thought by many that what He wrote was something that revealed the sins of the accusers. After her accusers had crept away one by one, Jesus asked her, "'Woman, where are those thine accusers? hath no man condemned thee?' She said, 'No man, Lord.' And Jesus said unto her, 'Neither do I condemn thee: go, and sin no more'" (John 8:10, 11).

Jesus, the revelation of the character of God to humanity, showed us, through His encounter with an adulteress and her accusers, that God's attitude toward sinners is one of simple and complete love and forgiveness. We may not *feel* that He is relating to us that way, but faith is not feeling. Our job is to believe that God loves us and has forgiven us in spite of our sin, no matter how dark that sin may be. This must be our belief about God, whether we feel it is true or not. Believing in God's changeless love in direct opposition to our feelings is a battle against self. This is the fight of faith. Think about this woman: Had she confessed her sins yet? No. Did she know Jesus was the Saviour? No. Had she prayed the sinner's prayer? No.

The forgiveness in God's heart not only preceded the cross, it also preceded any response of faith and repentance on our part. This type of forgiveness refers to what God feels toward sinners. God's goodness is what leads us to repentance. It is there before any response we make to Him.

So is there a word translated as "forgiveness" that describes forgiveness on the part of God the forgiver? Yes, it is the Greek word *charizomai* (Strong's G5483).

Uses: forgive 11; give 6; freely give 2; deliver 2; grant 1; frankly forgive 1. Total: 23.

Meanings:
- to do something pleasant or agreeable (to one), to do a favor to, gratify
- to show one's self gracious, kind, benevolent
- to grant forgiveness, to pardon
- to give graciously, give freely, bestow

Let's look at some verses that use *charizomai*.

"And you, being dead in your sins and the uncircumcision of your flesh, hath he quickened together with him, having forgiven you all trespasses" (Col. 2:13).

God has granted you *charizomai*. When? When you were dead in your sins. Was that before confession on your part? Yes.

Where has that forgiveness, that *charizomai*, taken place? In whose heart? *Charizomai* happens in God's heart.

"And be ye kind one to another, tenderhearted, forgiving one another, even as God for Christ's sake hath forgiven you" (Eph. 4:32).

Has God already forgiven you, according to this verse? Yes. Consider the logic of the following verse: "So that contrariwise ye ought rather to forgive him, and comfort him, lest perhaps such a one should be swallowed up with overmuch sorrow" (2 Cor. 2:7).

If you forgive someone else, that forgiveness is taking place in your heart, right? Whether or not it affects the heart of the one being forgiven, it must happen in your heart for you to forgive them. Can you comfort someone at whom you are still steaming mad? No, you have to have *charizomai* first. You have to have forgiveness in your heart.

Here is a little test to see if you understand the distinction between the two parts of this process. Look at this passage: "To whom ye forgive any thing, I *forgive* also: for if I forgave any thing, to whom I forgave it, for your sakes forgave I it in the person of Christ" (2 Cor. 2:10, italics supplied).

The second "forgive" (which I italicized) was inserted by the translators, but it was inserted because it is clearly implied that it must be the same form of forgiveness since it says "I forgive also." Paul is speaking of doing the same thing as the ones he is writing to.

"To whom ye forgive any thing ..." The question is, which "forgive" is this? Is it *charizomai* or *aphiemi/apoluo*? Is it forgiveness happening in the heart of the forgiver or the forgivee?

If you chose *charizomai*, forgiveness on the part of the forgiver, you made the right choice. You likely answered that way because it says "ye forgive." But there is another reason. There are many verses that mention forgiveness from God in which the texts are referring to what happens in the heart of the forgivee.

If you (the forgiver) forgive someone (the forgivee) who has wronged you and that forgiveness is *aphiemi/apoluo*, then what has happened in the forgivee? The guilt and shame are removed. Then can Paul, who is speaking in this verse, or anyone else come along and remove guilt and shame? No, it is already gone. You can't remove something that is not there.

Part 5: How are Sin and Forgiveness Related?

Let's look at some more quotes on forgiveness to see how these two aspects of forgiveness work together. Colossians 2 has lots to say about forgiveness: "When you were dead in your transgressions and the uncircumcision of your flesh, He made you alive together with Him, having forgiven us all our transgressions, having canceled out the certificate of debt consisting of decrees against us, which was hostile to us; and He has taken it out of the way, having nailed it to the cross" (Col. 2:13, 14, NASB).

For the moment, disregard the word "forgiven" and consider these questions:
- What is this "certificate of debt" that He canceled and nailed to His cross?
- From where was it taken?
- From whom and out of whose way did He take it?

What is the Certificate of Debt?

In the King James Version, Colossians 2:14 speaks of Christ "blotting out the handwriting of ordinances that was against us." The Greek word there for "handwriting" is *cheirographon* (khi-rog'-raf-on), which was a handwritten document that functioned as a promissory note. This was not referring to the law itself, but to a record of charges that stood against an individual, a record of their indebtedness. Therefore, canceling the debt is referring to God's act of taking our debt of sin and blotting it out.

From Where Was It Taken?

Specifically, from where was the debt taken? The prophet Jeremiah gives us a clue: "The sin of Judah is written with a pen of iron; with the point of a diamond it is engraved on the tablet of their heart" (Jer. 17:1, NKJV).

To what is the Bible referring by saying we have a record of sin in our heart? Simply that we have a conscience, which plagues us with guilt and condemnation when we understand our actions and behaviors to be inconsistent with what is right. The forgiveness on our part involves the canceling out of the record of our indebtedness and removing it from our consciences, thus setting us free from our inner guilt! God accomplished this miraculous change in us through our faith in the death of His Son. This was God's motive in giving Jesus to the world. Christ's death was not intended to appease any innate malice in God's heart or to get Him to forgive, but to liberate us from sin's psychological consequences and enable us to experience forgiveness. The following passage discusses this: "How much more shall the blood of Christ, who through the eternal Spirit offered Himself without spot to God, cleanse your conscience from dead works to serve the living God?" (Heb. 9:14, NKJV).

The blood of Christ cleanses our consciences from the guilt of our "dead works," works that lead to death. We are no longer bothered by a guilty conscience. The guilt and shame is gone. What wonderful relief! It changes us, not Him!

"Without shedding of blood there is no remission" (Heb. 9:22, NKJV).

The word "remission" does not refer to the forgiveness that occurs in God's heart. We have already noted that God forgave us in His great heart before any blood was shed. Had God not already forgiven us, no blood would have ever been shed to atone for sin. "Remission" here is translated from a form of the word *aphiemi* and is talking about the sinner's psychological freedom from the guilt of sin. The same word is used in this verse: "John came baptizing in the wilderness and preaching a baptism of repentance for the remission of sins" (Mark 1:4, NKJV).

Baptism is not about water cleansing the surface of the skin. The work of baptism goes deep, through our identification with the death, burial and resurrection of Jesus, to the work of cleansing our conscience. Baptism is meant to help us identify with the death, burial and resurrection of Jesus—that's why biblical baptism is in the form of immersion. You go under the water (burial) and are raised (resurrected) out of the water.

"And baptism, of which this [Noah's flood] is an image, now gives you salvation, not by washing clean the flesh, but by making you free from the sense of sin before God, through the coming again of Jesus Christ from the dead" (1 Pet. 3:21, BBE).

The King James Version speaks of this as "a good conscience toward God."

From Whom and Out of Whose Way Did He Take It?

By doing this grand work in us, Jesus took our indebtedness "out of the way." Out of whose way? Consider these questions: Have you ever owed someone something and couldn't pay it back? Did it get in the way of your relationship with them? When you saw them, did you intentionally turn the other way or at least avoid the topic of the debt?

Without the cross, our indebtedness would have prevented us from ever drawing close to the Father. Not because the Father would have held our debt over us or turned the other way, but because our enormous guilt would have loomed before us whenever we encountered Him. Our debt would still be in our way. We could never come near to Him because of the guilt of our indebtedness to Him. Jesus died to save us. He was crucified for us. It was for our redemption, and so that our debt could be taken away from us, that He took our certificate of debt and nailed it to His cross.

So God took our certificate of debt out of our way by putting it on Jesus and permitting Him to suffer the consequences instead of us. Why did He do this? Because in His heart, He had already forgiven us on an emotional level–*charizomai*. So look again at Colossians 2: "When you were dead in your transgressions and the uncircumcision of your flesh, He made you alive together with Him, having forgiven us all our transgressions, having canceled out the certificate of debt consisting of decrees against us, which was hostile to us; and He has taken it out of the way, having nailed it to the cross" (Col. 2:13, 14, NASB).

These verses indicate that God has already forgiven the trespasses of those who are still dead in transgressions, which sounds as though it happens before confession and repentance. So what is the word translated as "forgiven" in Colossians 2:13? *Charizomai.* The apostle John also talks about forgiveness in this well-known verse: "If we confess our sins, he is faithful and just to forgive us our sins, and to cleanse us from all unrighteousness" (1 John 1:9).

John is not talking here about the forgiveness that takes place within God's heart. We are not to think that God's heart is closed to sinners until they confess. Many believe and teach this unjust charge against God. He does not hold man at arm's length until we take the first step toward reconciliation. God freely forgave us from the tenderness of His heart long before we had even the first thought of confessing anything. This verse is referring to the work of canceling out our indebtedness, our sin and unrighteousness;

it happens in us, not in Him. And therefore it uses the word *aphiemi*, which is translated as "forgiveness."

Take note of what the verse itself is saying: "to cleanse us from all unrighteousness." This forgiveness centers, once again, on the cleansing work that God is doing in us. It's a matter of seeing our need to have the guilt and shame removed and choosing to allow God to do this for us. It happens in our minds, and God will not interfere with what happens there. He will do this work only if we allow Him.

"For if ye forgive men their trespasses, your heavenly Father will also forgive you: But if ye forgive not men their trespasses, neither will your Father forgive your trespasses" (Matt. 6:14, 15).

The word translated "forgive" here is *aphiemi*, not *charizomai*. If we *aphiemi* others, where is that forgiveness happening? Remember, it is also a two-party process when we forgive others. This verse is not referring to a change happening in us. How do we know? Because *aphiemi* describes the state of the forgivee. We may have a part in it, but the actual word *"aphiemi"* refers to forgiveness as they receive it. How do we know this refers to the removal of guilt and shame from the forgivee?

If we don't *aphiemi* others, does God forgive us? Yes, He forgives; He has given us *charizomai*, but we will not receive *aphiemi*. Why not? Because we cannot feel free of guilt and shame in our hearts if we are not willing to do what we should and need to in order for others to experience that freedom when they have wronged us.

Can you see the deeper meaning that comes from having more than one word for forgiveness?

There is another word that is used in relation to this topic, and it is closely related to the feelings of forgiveness. The word "remission" is translated from the Greek word *aphesis* (Strong's G859) and is derived from the word *aphiemi*. Note that in the following verse, remission is received, not granted: "To him give all the prophets witness, that through his name whosoever believeth in him shall receive remission of sins" (Acts 10:43).

There seem to be conditions attached to the remission of sin, as suggested by these verses:

"For this is my blood of the new testament, which is shed for many for the remission of sins" (Matt. 26:28).

"And almost all things are by the law purged with blood; and without shedding of blood is no remission" (Heb. 9:22).

Biblical Forgiveness

However, this shedding of blood is not conditional upon humans. Human beings do not have to shed their own blood to receive remission of sins. The blood of a Substitute was shed on their behalf.

Part 6: Pray to Receive, Not for God to Grant, Forgiveness

By now, I hope you can understand what a prayer for forgiveness of sins is actually a prayer for. Many who seek forgiveness feel guilty because, in their understanding, God has not forgiven them. In their thinking, there has to be a change in the heart of God toward them before the forgiveness can happen. Such thinking on our part should never keep us from asking for forgiveness.

I hope this study is increasing your understanding of what is involved in forgiveness. A misunderstanding of biblical forgiveness is one of the greatest reasons why people stay away from God. Maybe you have felt that you were not good enough or that you needed to get your act together for God to accept you. Please understand that forgiveness is a two-party transaction.

On God's side, He has already forgiven you in His heart. He does not need to change His attitude toward you. He has always loved you and has provided the means to remove the guilt and shame from you—so you can feel forgiven—long before you were even born.

On your side, understand that feeling forgiven does not come from a change in God's attitude toward you; it comes from first realizing that He has forgiven you, and then you doing anything needed to remove the guilt and shame, such as stopping a sinful action. Confessing your sins includes realizing that you are involved in sin and turning from it, forsaking it. When you are no longer involved in sin, there is no reason for guilt and shame; the sin that causes it is gone. Guilt and shame are natural consequences of wrong actions. Stop the action that causes guilt and shame, and the guilt and shame stops. Is that simple enough?

God does not change. God is love. Therefore, everything He does has to be consistent with what He is. He treats us in a different way because we have changed course. The change in His actions is because He does not change—He is love and always will be love. He always does what is loving, but what is loving may change as the circumstances change. He always loves us and puts us before Himself. He always forgives us *(charizomai)*. But if we will not allow Him to take away the guilt and shame, then forgiveness *(apheimi)*—that release from feelings of guilt and shame—doesn't happen in us. But in His heart He still loves and forgives us and will ultimately do the most loving thing He can for those who do not accept forgiveness. Ultimately, He mercifully allows unrepentant sinners to die the second death.

Two-party Transaction Expanded

I mentioned at the start that forgiveness is a two-party transaction with a forgiver and a forgivee. I would like to clarify that a little. While there are two sides involved, the two processes are a little more independent of each other than one might see at first glance.

What do you expect to happen in answer to a prayer for forgiveness of sins? We need to realize that God, in His heart, has already forgiven us whether we accept it or not, whether we know it or not, even whether we want it or not. His forgiveness, His *charizomai* does not depend upon our being good enough, and it does not depend on our repentance or confession or even upon us feeling like we are lousy sinners. He continues to love us, to offer us His blessing, and even to bless us. He desperately wants you to be saved eternally and to turn to Him today. He wants to increase your understanding so you will realize the depth of His acceptance and love for you.

Now that you understand forgiveness, pray intelligently when you ask for forgiveness. Don't pray for God to *charizomai* you because He already has. People pray "Please, please, God; please forgive me." They beg and plead and promise: "Dear God, if You'll just forgive me, I won't do it again." And they think of and look for a change in God. "God, please will You [stop being mad at me and] forgive me?" Don't do that—He already has forgiven you. Don't plead for *charizomai* to happen; it happened long ago.

The other choice when praying for forgiveness is to pray that God will *aphiemi* you, that He will take away the guilt and shame from your heart. But what is needed for that to happen? You need to stop doing the sin, and you need to make it right with God or whoever is involved. The guilt and shame is a consequence of your wrong actions. So quit the actions! The focus of your prayer really needs to be recognition of how good and merciful and forgiving God is and always has been, and how you need to change.

Let's look again at the verse with which we started this study: "But thou art a God ready to pardon ..." (Neh. 9:17). Being ready to pardon, of course, is the same as the forgiver granting forgiveness.

Now a final test. What is He ready to do, stop being mad at you? No. Forgive you in His heart? No, He has already done that. He is ready to take the shame and guilt away from you the moment you will let Him.

Part 6: Pray to Receive, Not for God to Grant, Forgiveness

The word "pardon" here is a variation of the Hebrew word *calach* which is equivalent to the Greek *aphiemi*. I think if you understand how this works—what has already happened on God's side, in His heart toward you, which is *charizomai* forgiveness—you will be greatly encouraged to go forward, and with His help, to deal with things in your life so that you will truly experience *aphiemi* forgiveness in your own heart.

 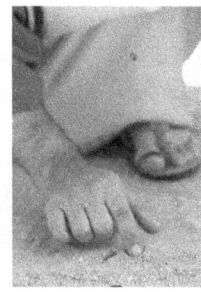

While the law, which was designed to protect us, was written in stone to show its permanence, Jesus wrote the sins of the accusers of the adulteress in the dust of the ground to show how ready God was to erase them.

Biblical Forgiveness

Part 7: The Blotting Out of Sins

There is one other aspect of forgiveness that we should look at. What does it mean to blot out sins or names? How does this relate to the forgiveness of sins? Previously, we have seen that forgiveness and related words in the Bible refer to what is essentially an emotional transaction—a matter of feeling or attitude. The question of our legal status, whether we are saved or lost and whether or not our names are still in the book of life, is another matter. We often think of forgiveness in that way, but is this correct? Read the verses carefully and you will find that the words "forgiveness," "forgiven," and so on are used more in terms of the attitude or emotions of the forgiver or the forgivee. The legal status, related more to the state of salvation, is covered by terms such as "blotted out." Here we will examine "blotting out" and similar terms, and their use in scripture.

Uses of "blot [out]" as a verb in the Old Testament are all translated from the Hebrew word *machah* (Strong's H4229).

Uses: (blot, put, etc.) out 17; destroy 6; wipe 4; blot 3; wipe away 2; abolished 1; marrow 1; reach 1; utterly 1. Total: 36.

Meanings (some):
- to wipe, wipe out
- to wipe
- to blot out, obliterate
- to blot out, exterminate
- to blot out (from memory)
- to strike

"Blot" as a noun (as in a blemish) is translated two times from the Hebrew word *moom* (Strong's H3971).

Uses: blemish 16; spot 3; blot 2; variant 1. Total: 22.

Meanings:
- blemish, spot, defect
- of physical defect
- of moral stain

In the New Testament, three uses of the Greek word *exaleipho* (Strong's G1813) are translated as "blotted out" (Acts 3:19), "blotting out" (Col. 2:14), and "blot out" (Rev. 3:5), and all have reference to a written record of something being removed.

Uses: blot out 3; wipe away 2. Total: 5.

Meanings:
- to anoint or wash in every part
- to besmear: i.e., cover with lime (to whitewash or plaster)
- to wipe off, wipe away
- to obliterate, erase, wipe out, blot out

The other two uses of the word *exaleipho* refer to wiping away tears.

From the uses of "blot out," it is apparent that that action is an act of removing sins and/or names from records. It is not a matter of feeling or emotion but more of a legal matter. For God to blot out the record of our sins and retain our names in the book of life, there are conditions.

"Neither is there salvation in any other: for there is none other name under heaven given among men, whereby we must be saved" (Acts 4:12).

But His feelings of love and forgiveness, of not holding any feelings of dislike or vindictiveness towards sinners, do not have conditions. He totally loves saint and sinner alike. Compare this concept of blotting out sins to the meaning of words used for forgiveness and I think you will find that those words are speaking about something different than the legal issue of the record of sin being blotted out.

Summary

God always forgives you from His heart. He does not hold a grudge or unforgiving feelings toward you while waiting for you to do something first. This is a wonderful truth that will increase your love for Him. Realizing His true feelings toward you makes it much easier to accept the freely-offered salvation that will result in even the record of your sins being blotted out.

And it makes sense when compared to our experience. Think especially of the parents of young children. They always forgive their children when they do something wrong; they don't love them any less, and they don't hold grudges against them. Children help teach us of the relationship between God and us and how He regards us.

So accept the forgiveness that is freely offered to you. Learn to see God as the wonderful parent He is. Isn't it a blessing to understand God's forgiveness? Rejoice in His free forgiveness and the removal of your feelings of guilt!

We invite you to view the complete
selection of titles we publish at:

www.TEACHServices.com

Scan with your mobile
device to go directly
to our website.

Please write or email us your praises, reactions, or
thoughts about this or any other book we publish at:

TEACH Services, Inc.
P U B L I S H I N G
www.TEACHServices.com

P.O. Box 954
Ringgold, GA 30736

info@TEACHServices.com

TEACH Services, Inc., titles may be purchased in bulk for
educational, business, fund-raising, or sales promotional use.
For information, please e-mail:

BulkSales@TEACHServices.com

Finally, if you are interested in seeing
your own book in print, please contact us at

publishing@TEACHServices.com

We would be happy to review your manuscript for free.

www.ingramcontent.com/pod-product-compliance
Lightning Source LLC
Chambersburg PA
CBHW031659040426
42453CB00006B/349